MIND SET OF LEGENDS
How to Achieve Anything
you
want in Life

For permission requests, write to the publisher at the address below:

Trio

India

triangletrio9117@gmail.com

www.Triangletriobook.com

ISBN: 9798868348976

Imprint: Independently published

CONTENTS

INTRODUCTION

The Legendary Mindset In the vast tapestry of human history, certain individuals stand out as luminous beacons of inspiration and innovation. They are the legends, the trailblazers, and the visionaries who have shaped our world with their extraordinary thinking and actions. What sets them apart is not mere chance or inherent genius, but a mindset—a legendary mindset.

"The Legendary Mindset" is an exploration of this exceptional way of thinking, a journey through the essence of what makes these individuals legendary. It's a voyage into the depths of curiosity, resilience, and the unwavering commitment to leaving a lasting legacy. Whether you're a seasoned professional or just beginning to chart your course, this book invites you to embrace the legendary mindset and embark on a quest for personal and collective greatness.

Throughout the pages of this book, you will traverse the landscape of legendary thinking, guided by ten distinct chapters, each unveiling a unique facet of the legendary mindset. From cultivating curiosity to persevering beyond a lifetime, you'll gain insights, knowledge, and actionable steps to propel your own journey to legendary thinking.

As you delve into the chapters, remember that legendary thinking is not confined to history books or distant memories; it is a living, breathing philosophy that anyone can adopt. The legendary mindset knows no boundaries of age, background, or profession. It is a blueprint for a life of   significance,   an unending quest for growth and the empowerment of those who come after us.

Let this book serve as your guide and companion as you embark on your own legendary journey. The pages that follow are not just words on paper; they are the keys to unlocking your potential and leaving an enduring legacy. Welcome to the realm of "The Legendary Mindset."

Book Summary

In a world shadowed by ambiguity and division, the clandestine Trio emerges as the beacon of change, their identities concealed, their purpose unyielding. "Understanding the Legendary Mindset" isn't just a book; it's a revolutionary manifesto, the first in a series that promises to redefine masculinity, femininity, and the very essence of human unity.

Embark on a journey guided by the enigmatic Trio, architects of a literary uprising. This isn't merely a narrative; it's a call to arms, challenging societal norms and advocating for the revival of true manhood and womanhood. Trio asserts a simple truth – there are only two genders, and each person deserves respect for their beliefs and identity.

The book unfolds like a rebellion against stagnation, inviting readers to defy expectations, shatter preconceptions, and embrace the radical idea that unity is the ultimate power. Trio extends an invitation to join a movement that transcends literature's conventional boundaries.

As you turn the pages, the words become a declaration: every reader possesses the potential to become a legend. The Trio beckons, inviting you to be a part of a literary revolution that goes beyond the ordinary. This isn't just a book; it's the prelude to an extraordinary journey, a compelling narrative that leaves you eager for the next chapter in the Trio's revolutionary series. Prepare to be captivated, enlightened, and inspired. The revolution begins here.

NOTE TO READERS

Dear Reader,

In "The Legendary Mindset," you'll find a collection of insights and strategies drawn from the wealth of human experience and wisdom. This book aims to impact your life by offering practical tools to navigate challenges, foster resilience, and embrace a mindset that leads to extraordinary changes.

May these words inspire transformative shifts in your thinking, guiding you toward a life marked by resilience, triumph over adversity, and the pursuit of legendary greatness.

Wishing you a journey of profound change,

Understanding the Legendary Mindset

CONTENTS

Chapter 1: Understanding the Legendary Mindset

Introduction

 Welcome to the foundational journey of cultivating a mindset that transcends the ordinary and paves the way for the extraordinary—The Legendary Mindset. In Sub-Chapter 1.1, we delve deep into the essence of what it means to foster a legendary mindset, exploring the very roots from which this transformative thinking sprouts. We'll delve into the core concepts that will guide us through the rest of this journey.

we've made each chapter into 5 part for you to understand and take in more. note that each chapter and sub chapter will be small for you better understanding

Sub-Chapter 1.1: The Power of Mindset

Introduction

Your mindset is the lens through which you perceive and interact with the world. In this sub-chapter, we'll explore the profound influence of mindset on your thoughts, behaviors, and outcomes.

The Influence of Mindset

Your mindset isn't just a passive aspect of your personality; it actively shapes your reality. The way you think about yourself, your abilities, and the world around you can be a self-fulfilling prophecy.

A fixed mindset, characterized by the belief that abilities and traits are set in stone, can limit your potential. On the other hand, a growth mindset, where you see abilities as malleable and can be developed through effort, leads to greater resilience and achievement.

Understanding Fixed and Growth Mindsets

Fixed Mindset: This mindset assumes that intelligence, talent, and abilities are innate and unchangeable. Failure is seen as a reflection of one's inherent limitations.

Growth Mindset: This mindset believes that intelligence, talent, and abilities can be developed through dedication and hard work. Failure is viewed as an opportunity for growth and learning.

The Impact on Success

Your mindset has a significant impact on your ability to succeed. Individuals with a growth mindset tend to embrace challenges, persist in the face of setbacks, and see effort as a path to mastery. They are more likely to achieve their goals and reach their full potential.

Cultivating a Growth Mindset

We'll discuss practical strategies for cultivating a growth mindset, such as: Embracing challenges and viewing them as opportunities for growth. Learning from failures and setbacks rather than being discouraged by them. Effort and dedication as the keys to improvement.

By the end of this sub-chapter, you'll have a deeper understanding of how your mindset can be your greatest asset in your pursuit of a legendary life

Sub-Chapter 1.2: Shaping Your Beliefs

Introduction

Our beliefs act as the foundation upon which our mindset is built. In this sub-chapter, we will explore how you can actively shape your beliefs to foster a growth-oriented mindset and encourage legendary thinking.

The Role of Beliefs

Your beliefs are the stories you tell yourself about your abilities, potential, and the world. They shape your thoughts, emotions, and behaviors, often unconsciously. Understanding and influencing your beliefs is the first step to adopting a legendary mindset.

Identifying Your Current Beliefs

We'll guide you through the process of recognizing your existing beliefs, including both empowering and limiting ones.

Self-awareness is key to reshaping your mindset. You'll learn to pinpoint beliefs that may be holding you back.

Challenging Limiting Beliefs

Many beliefs are self-imposed limitations that can be overcome .We'll explore practical techniques to challenge and reframe limiting beliefs into empowering ones.

The Power of Affirmations

Self-affirmations can be a valuable tool for altering your beliefs. Discover how to create and use positive affirmations effectively.

In your armory lies the art of self-affirmation, a potent chisel for remolding beliefs. Unearth the craft of fashioning and effectively wielding positive affirmations to craft your mindset.

Visualization and Belief Reinforcement

Visualization emerges as a potent tool for reinforcing affirmative beliefs. Uncover the cryptic methods of visualization and learn how to wield it effectively to bolster the bastions of your legendary mindset.

As you tread through this sub-chapter, you'll acquire a treasury of strategies to consciously shape your beliefs in harmonious resonance with the legendary mindset, much like a master architect erecting an enduring masterpiece..

By the end of this sub-chapter, you'll have a toolbox of strategies to consciously shape your beliefs in a way that aligns with the legendary mindset.

Sub-Chapter 1.3: Breaking the Chains of Limiting Beliefs

Introduction

In the vast landscape of personal development, few obstacles loom larger than limiting beliefs—a subtle yet potent force that shackles us from realizing our fullest potential. Welcome to Sub-Chapter 1.3, where we embark on a profound exploration into the depths of these constricting thoughts. Here, we not only identify the common limiting beliefs that encumber many but arm you with actionable strategies to shatter their constraints.

Unveiling the Veil: Identifying Common Limiting Beliefs

The journey begins with a revealing discussion on the pervasive limiting beliefs that silently weave their influence into our lives. We dissect these beliefs, exposing them to the light of awareness. Identifying these subtle saboteurs within your own mindset is the inaugural stride toward emancipation.

The Weight of Chains: The Impact of Limiting Beliefs

Limiting beliefs, like heavy chains, possess the capacity to stifle personal and professional growth. We navigate through the intricate ways these beliefs metamorphose into self-fulfilling prophecies, constructing barriers that thwart the realization of your most cherished goals.

A Symphony of Liberation: Strategies for Overcoming Limiting Beliefs

Prepare to equip yourself with a repertoire of practical and transformative strategies. These methods serve as a symphony of liberation, empowering you to challenge and reconstruct the very fabric of your limiting beliefs. Each strategy is a note contributing to the melody of a more empowering, growth-oriented mindset.

The Looking Glass: The Role of Self-Awareness

A crucial facet in this transformative journey is self-awareness. Together, we delve into the reflective looking glass of self-awareness, where understanding yourself and your beliefs becomes the catalyst for profound change. Here, awareness isn't just a tool; it's the mirror reflecting the potential for positive transformation.

Rising from the Ashes: Cultivating a Growth Mindset

The essence of overcoming limiting beliefs intertwines with the adoption of a growth mindset. Discover how shedding the weight of these mental limitations isn't merely liberation—it's the phoenix rising from the ashes of self-imposed constraints. As you cultivate a growth mindset, the stage is set for a metamorphosis—a transformation that extends beyond personal boundaries into the realm of professional and personal excellence.

As we navigate the expanses of this sub-chapter, envision it not only as a guide but as a catalyst for your journey toward a legendary mindset. Break free from the chains, embrace the transformation, and step into the realm of limitless possibilities.

Sub-Chapter 1.4: Cultivating Resilience: The Indomitable Heart of Legends

Introduction

In our relentless journey to embrace the legendary mindset, we embark on a profound exploration of resilience, the unyielding anchor that guides legends through the tempestuous seas of life.

Resilience: The Unseen Anchor

Resilience stands as the invisible anchor that keeps legends steady in the face of life's most ferocious storms. It is the unwavering force that allows them to bend without breaking, adapting with grace to the ever-changing tides of life's tumultuous waters.

Navigating Life's Storms: Challenges as Catalysts

Challenges are not mere roadblocks but powerful catalysts for growth on the path to legendary thinking. Legends confront these tempests with unyielding determination, recognizing that they possess the power to emerge from the tempests stronger and more resolute.

Transforming Setbacks into Triumphs

Resilience transcends mere survival; it is a triumphant resurgence. Legends view setbacks as stepping stones to personal growth and innovation, refusing to surrender to defeat. They transform adversity into a powerful force for renewal.

A Mindset of Triumph: Resilience as a Way of Life

Resilience is more than just a trait; it is a way of life. It empowers legendary thinkers to not only withstand change but to thrive in its midst, emerging not as mere survivors but as victors, regardless of circumstances.

As you dive into this sub-chapter, you'll gain profound insights into how resilience serves as a perpetual force on the path to legendary thinking, much like an anchor securing a ship through the most tumultuous seas of life, keeping the legend's heart unshaken and unwavering.

Sub-Chapter 1.5: Embracing the Essence of Self-Compassion

Introduction

Embark on an immersive exploration of profound self-nurturing within the legendary mindset as we journey through the expansive landscapes of Sub-Chapter 1.5. Here, the narrative unfolds around the priceless essence of self-compassion—an indispensable element not only fostering personal growth but profoundly influencing overall well-being.

Understanding the Depths of Self-Compassion

Initiate the odyssey by delving into the nuanced concept of self-compassion, a practice rooted in the tender embrace of kindness and understanding. Particularly poignant during life's challenging junctures, explore the multifaceted components that intricately weave together, forming the rich tapestry of self-compassion. Unveil its pivotal role as a guiding force in the ongoing journey of personal development.

Dispelling the Illusion of Self-Criticism

Challenge the prevailing myth that self-criticism serves as the sole driving force behind achievement. Unearth the profound truth that self-compassion stands not only as a more effective motivator but as a sustainable and nurturing force on your legendary journey.

Empowering Through Self-Affirmations

Embark on an illuminating quest to uncover the transformative power inherent in self-affirmations—positive statements meticulously crafted to fortify the very bedrock of self-compassion. Delve into the intricate interplay of science and practice that renders self-affirmations formidable tools, fostering a compassionate and affirming relationship with oneself.

Cultivating the Seeds of Self-Compassion

Embark on a comprehensive odyssey through a rich array of practical techniques. These are thoughtfully designed to sow the seeds of self-compassion into the fertile soil of your daily life. This section stands as a detailed roadmap, offering a tapestry of exercises and strategies, enhancing your capacity for profound kindness and understanding towards yourself.

Vision and goal setting

CONTENTS

2.1: Defining Your Vision

At the core of legendary thinking lies a vibrant vision—an image of your future that kindles your soul. Through introspection and reflection, embark on a journey to define a vision that becomes the cornerstone of your legendary aspirations.

2.2: Setting Meaningful Goals

Goals are the stepping stones to greatness, translating your vision into actionable steps. Learn the art of setting goals that resonate with your core values and deepest desires, transforming tasks into tangible manifestations of your vision.

2.3: Creating a Vision Board

Visualization breathes life into dreams. Craft a vision board, a tangible representation of your vision through images and words. This artistic creation keeps your aspirations vividly present in your daily life.
2.4: Daily Habits for Goal Achievement
Achieving goals requires consistent effort. Discover daily habits and routines supporting your journey, from effective time management to cultivating discipline. These habits are the threads weaving the fabric of your success.

2.5: Navigating Setbacks

Setbacks are not roadblocks but opportunities for growth. Develop the skill of navigating setbacks, learning strategies to stay on course even in the face of challenges. This mastery is essential for every legendary individual on their path to greatness.

Chapter 2: Vision and goal setting

Introduction

Embark on an odyssey within the legendary mindset with Chapter 2, where the very fabric of your journey to greatness unfolds. At its core lies a compelling vision—an alluring destination that calls you forth.

This vision is not just a point on the horizon; it's the North Star of your life, casting a radiant and guiding light upon your path. In this expansive chapter, we embark on a profound exploration, unraveling the pivotal role of vision and delving into the intricate artistry of goal setting. This journey is your canvas, and the strokes of vision and goals paint the masterpiece of your legendary existence.

Sub-Chapter 2.1: The Guiding Radiance - Defining Your Vision

Introduction

In the heart of a legendary mindset, a vision burns like an unwavering beacon in the vast darkness. This is no mere abstract dream; it's a vivid mental image, a lighthouse illuminating the future you aspire to create. Your vision serves as more than inspiration; it's the driving force propelling you forward, resilient even in the face of adversity.

Embarking on the Inner Quest

Your journey to define your vision commences with introspection. Dive into the depths of your desires, passions, and core values. Pose questions that unveil your deepest convictions. What truly matters to you? What legacy do you wish to imprint upon the world? This introspection forms the cornerstone of your vision.

Crafting a Vision that Resonates

Once the recesses of your desires and values are unearthed, you can meticulously craft a vision resonating with the very essence of your soul. This vision transcends external success; it encapsulates the fulfillment of your innermost aspirations and the positive contribution you yearn to make to the world.

Vision as Your Guiding Compass

A well-defined vision acts as your unwavering compass, imparting direction to your actions and decisions. It infuses clarity and purpose into your life, serving as a constant reminder of your destination. With a defined vision, you cease to be a mere passenger on this journey; you become the captain of your destiny.

Moving Forward with Your Vision

As you navigate your legendary journey, your vision becomes a steadfast companion, anchoring you on the path to greatness. It's more than motivation;

it's the force propelling your endeavors and aiding you in surmounting the challenges that loom ahead.

A Deeper Narrative Journey

This sub-chapter isn't just a guide; it's an immersive portal into the profound realms where your aspirations crystallize into the foundational essence of your legendary journey

Sub-Chapter 2.2: Navigating the Path - Setting Meaningful Goals

Introduction

In the intricate tapestry of your legendary journey, goals emerge as the stepping stones bridging the chasm between vision and reality. They are not mere markers but transformative agents, turning aspirations into tangible plans that guide you toward the realization of your vision.

The Essence of Meaningful Goals

Meaningful goals transcend the realm of mere checklists or resolutions; they are the heartbeat of your vision translated into actionable objectives. Aligned with your deepest desires and values, these goals infuse purpose into your every action.

Exploration of Meaningful Goals

Imagine your meaningful goals as dynamic vessels navigating the expansive waters of your aspirations. These goals, when imbued with significance, become vessels that carry the essence of your vision, steering your journey toward greatness.

A Soulful Translation of Vision

Embarking on the journey to set meaningful goals, it's crucial to grasp that these goals are not imposed by external expectations. Instead, they emanate from your innermost desires and aspirations. When your goals resonate deeply with meaning, they transform into the compass directing your actions and shaping your choices.

Unraveling the Compass

Your compass of meaningful goals is more than a navigational tool; it's an intimate guide. It signifies goals deeply connected to your vision, aligning your actions with your core values. As you navigate through this sub-chapter, envision your meaningful goals as points on the compass, guiding you steadfastly toward the epicenter of your legendary journey.

Empowerment Through Goals

Delve into the empowerment offered by meaningful goals. They aren't mere checkpoints; they are sources of strength, infusing each step with purpose and determination. In this exploration, recognize the transformative power of your goals as they propel you toward the zenith of your legendary aspirations.

Sub-Chapter 2.3: Crafting Your Visual Compass - Creating a Vision Board

Introduction

In the realm of legendary thinking, a vision board emerges as a potent instrument, transforming abstract aspirations into a tangible, daily guide. This collage of images, words, and symbols serves as a visual representation of the life you envision, weaving your dreams into a vivid tapestry.

The Artistic Alchemy of Vision Board Creation

Crafting a vision board is not a mundane task; it's a creative and inspiring process. Delve into the art of selecting images and words that harmonize with your vision. Arrange them with intention, creating a visual narrative that resonates deeply. This process is not just an artistic endeavor; it's a soulful journey of emotional connection.

Placement as Intention - The Daily Visual Odyssey

Once your vision board takes shape, its placement is strategic. Situating it where you encounter it daily ensures that your vision remains a constant presence in your thoughts and actions. This intentional placement transforms your vision board from a mere collage into a daily guide, influencing your choices and guiding your journey.

The Vision Board as Motivational Dynamo

Your vision board is more than a collection of images; it's a dynamic source of motivation. It reinforces your commitment to your vision, keeping your goals in focus. Each glance at your vision board becomes a reminder of the

life you are diligently crafting. It transcends being a static collage; it becomes a living, breathing part of your daily experience.

Transforming Dreams into Reality

As you explore the creation of your visual compass in this sub-chapter, envision your vision board not merely as an artistic project but as a transformative force, aligning your daily experiences with the grandeur of your envisioned life. Through this transformative journey, your dreams cease to be distant aspirations; they become the guiding stars of your everyday reality.

Sub-Chapter 2.4: Navigating the Daily Seas - Daily Habits for Goal Achievement

Introduction

In the pursuit of legendary thinking, the seas of achievement are navigated not by occasional bursts of effort but by the steady wind of daily habits. This sub-chapter unfurls the sails of understanding, exploring the vital role of daily habits and routines in the sacred journey of goal achievement.

The Symphony of Daily Habits

Achieving greatness requires a symphony of consistent, purposeful actions. Legendary individuals recognize the harmonious melody played by daily habits in the grand orchestration of goal realization. These habits, ranging from effective time management to the cultivation of discipline, become the rhythmic beats that guide your journey.

The Craft of Time Management

Time is the currency of achievement, and its management is an art form. Delve into the craft of effective time management as a crucial daily habit. Learn how to allocate your time with intention, ensuring that each moment contributes meaningfully to your journey.

Discipline as the Guiding North Star

Discipline is the North Star that steers the ship of daily habits toward the destination of greatness. Explore the cultivation of discipline as an indispensable habit. Understand how discipline transforms your actions from mere tasks into purposeful steps on the path to your envisioned future.

Consistency as the Structural Foundation

Consistency forms the bedrock upon which greatness is built. Daily habits are not isolated actions but the consistent threads that weave the fabric of your success. Explore the profound impact of consistency in ensuring that your daily habits create a sturdy and reliable structure for your journey.

Embrace the Daily Rituals

As you embark on the exploration of daily habits in this sub-chapter, recognize them not as mere routines but as sacred rituals. Each habit becomes a ritualistic offering to the vision you hold dear, creating a daily tapestry that tells the story of your legendary journey. Through the embrace of these daily rituals, your path becomes illuminated, and your goals draw closer with every intentional step.

Sub-Chapter 2.5: Uncharted Waters - Navigating Setbacks

Introduction

In the saga of legendary thinking, setbacks are not ominous storms but uncharted waters waiting to be explored. This sub-chapter unfurls the sails of wisdom, guiding you through the intricate dance of setbacks and transforming them into stepping stones on your legendary journey.

Setbacks: The Unavoidable Ebb of the Journey

Setbacks, like the ebb and flow of the tide, are an inseparable part of any journey. Legendary individuals embrace setbacks not as impediments but as opportunities for growth and learning. This perspective shifts setbacks from being ominous clouds to becoming essential threads in the rich tapestry of greatness.

Strategies for Navigating Uncharted Waters

When confronted with setbacks, legends don't retreat; they navigate with resilience. Delve into practical strategies that help you maintain your course amid challenges. These strategies aren't just survival tools; they are instruments for thriving in the face of adversity. Learn how setbacks can become the very fuel that propels you forward on your legendary odyssey.

Resilience as the North Star

Resilience is the guiding North Star in the face of setbacks. Explore the art of cultivating resilience as a transformative strategy. Understand how resilience transforms setbacks from detours into scenic routes, each twist and turn offering valuable lessons for your growth.

Learning from the Storms

In the journey to greatness, setbacks aren't storms to be avoided but storms to be embraced. Each setback carries profound lessons. Explore how setbacks, when navigated with intention, become catalysts for learning and self-discovery. As you navigate these uncharted waters, you not only endure but emerge stronger, wiser, and more prepared for the adventures that lie ahead.

Setbacks as the Catalyst for Legendary Progress

As you immerse yourself in the exploration of setbacks in this sub-chapter, envision them not as stumbling blocks but as catalysts propelling you toward legendary progress. With each setback navigated, your journey becomes a testament to the resilience and fortitude that define a truly legendary mindset.

*Build confidence
and
self esteem*

CONTENTS

Chapter 3: The Inner Citadel - Building Confidence and Self-Esteem

Introduction

Within the realm of legendary thinking, confidence and self-esteem stand as sentinels, guarding the gates to greatness. This chapter unveils the profound role these twin pillars play in shaping your legendary journey. Confidence and self-esteem, far from being innate, are sculpted and nurtured, emerging from a profound understanding of your intrinsic worth and capabilities. As you delve into this chapter, witness how these qualities become the bedrock, allowing you to boldly tread the path toward your vision.

Sub-Chapter 3.1: Embracing Imperfections - Self-Acceptance and Confidence

Introduction

Embark on a transformative journey as we delve into the symbiotic relationship between self-acceptance and confidence. In this sub-chapter, we navigate the uncharted waters of embracing imperfections, understanding that self-acceptance is the cornerstone for building genuine confidence in the legendary mindset.

The Tapestry of Confidence Woven in Self-Acceptance

Self-acceptance, the genesis of confidence, is the art of embracing one's true self, flaws and all. This sub-chapter unfolds the narrative of how acknowledging and appreciating your authentic self becomes the catalyst for cultivating unwavering confidence. Prepare to navigate the intricacies of self-discovery and self-love.

Journeying through Setbacks: The Ebb and Flow of Confidence

Much like setbacks in legendary thinking, the ebb and flow of confidence are intertwined. Embrace setbacks not as adversaries but as essential elements in the tapestry of confidence-building. Learn how each challenge becomes a thread, weaving a resilient and confident mindset capable of weathering any storm on the path to greatness.

Strategies for Navigating Self-Discovery

As we explore the strategies for navigating the uncharted waters of self-discovery, consider them not merely as tools for survival but as instruments for thriving. Resilience, the guiding North Star, illuminates the way, transforming setbacks into opportunities for personal growth and legendary progress.

Learning and Progress as the Fruits of Self-Acceptance

In this sub-chapter, self-acceptance isn't just a destination; it's the catalyst for legendary progress. Each step taken in embracing imperfections and navigating setbacks becomes a testament to the resilience and fortitude embedded in the legendary mindset. As you navigate these uncharted waters, let self-acceptance be the compass guiding you toward unparalleled confidence and greatness.

Sub-Chapter 3.2: Cultivating the Growth Mindset

Introduction

Journey into the transformative realm of a growth mindset, where belief in the malleability of abilities becomes the cornerstone of confidence. In this concise sub-chapter, unravel the symbiotic connection between a growth mindset and the legendary journey, discovering how it becomes a catalyst for boosted confidence and empowered strides.

The Seeds of Confidence in Growth

A growth mindset is the fertile soil in which confidence blossoms. Explore the intricate dance of effort and perseverance that forms the core of this mindset. Understand how this belief not only cultivates abilities but also serves as the catalyst for a heightened sense of agency and control over your journey towards legendary achievements.

Navigating the Landscape of Abilities

Discover the practical aspects of adopting a growth mindset as you navigate the landscape of your abilities. This mindset isn't just a concept; it's a dynamic force that propels you forward. Strategies unfold as you delve into how embracing growth becomes the compass guiding your actions, boosting confidence with each step.

Empowering Your Legendary Journey

In this sub-chapter, a growth mindset isn't just a tool; it's the empowering force steering your legendary journey. As you explore the transformative potential of this mindset, envision how it becomes the wind in your sails, propelling you towards newfound confidence and untold greatness.

Unleashing Potential Through Growth

Embark on a journey of self-discovery and empowerment as you cultivate a growth mindset. Beyond a mere belief, this mindset becomes the fertile ground for confidence to flourish, guiding you through the evolving landscape of your abilities. Embrace the empowering essence of growth as you navigate your legendary journey, where each step is infused with the unstoppable momentum of a mindset poised for greatness.

Sub-Chapter 3.3: Confronting Shadows - Facing Fear and Building Courage

Introduction

Embark on a transformative exploration of fear and courage in the legendary mindset. Fear, a natural companion on life's journey, is not a barrier but a portal to growth. In this succinct sub-chapter, discover strategies to confront fear and build courage, understanding that true courage is not the absence of fear but the resolute willingness to act despite it.

Unveiling Fear's Mechanisms: Physiological and Psychological Triggers

Gain insights into the intricate workings of fear, both in the body and the mind. Explore the physiological and psychological mechanisms that trigger fear responses during challenging situations. This understanding serves as the foundation for effective strategies to control and manage fear on your legendary journey.

Strategies for Confronting Fear

Explore practical strategies that empower you to face your fears head-on. Legendary individuals don't evade fear; they confront it with intention. Discover how these strategies become the tools that dismantle the walls of fear, allowing you to move forward on your legendary odyssey.

Courage as the Catalyst

In this sub-chapter, courage is unveiled as the catalyst born from the confrontation with fear. True courage is not the absence of fear but the bold choice to act despite its presence. As you navigate the shadows of fear,

envision each courageous step as a testament to the indomitable spirit of a legendary mindset.

Empowered Action in the Face of Fear

In facing fear and building courage, the legendary mindset emerges as a beacon of empowered action. Each strategy becomes a step towards breaking the shackles of fear, transforming it into fuel for your journey. Embrace the power of courage as you tread the path where fear becomes the fertile ground for legendary progress.

Sub-Chapter 3.4: Embracing Evaluations - Handling Criticism with Legendary Grace

Introduction

Enter the realm where criticism transforms from a deterrent to a catalyst for growth. In the legendary mindset, handling criticism is an art—a dance that embraces evaluations with grace and resilience. In this focused sub-chapter, unravel the strategies that not only shield you from the sting of criticism but also empower you to leverage it for personal growth.

Decoding the Nature of Criticism

Understand that criticism, like a double-edged sword, has both constructive and destructive potential. Delve into the intricacies of evaluating criticism, distinguishing between feedback aimed at improvement and negativity that seeks to hinder your progress. This discernment is the first step in handling criticism with legendary finesse.

Responding with Grace and Resilience

Legendary individuals don't react impulsively to criticism; they respond with grace and resilience. Explore effective strategies for crafting responses that maintain your dignity while fostering an environment of open communication. Learn the art of extracting valuable insights from criticism, turning it into a stepping stone rather than a stumbling block.

Leveraging Criticism for Growth

In the legendary mindset, criticism becomes a tool for growth. Discover how to leverage constructive criticism to refine your skills and strategies. Embrace criticism not as a condemnation but as a guidepost, directing you toward

excellence on your legendary journey. With each encounter, transform criticism into a powerful force propelling you toward your aspirations.

Cultivating a Legendary Response

Crafting a legendary response to criticism involves more than words; it requires a mindset shift. Learn to view criticism not as a personal attack but as an opportunity for improvement. Develop the resilience to navigate through criticism, emerging stronger and more focused on your path to legendary greatness.

In this sub-chapter, handling criticism is not a defensive act but a transformative dance—a testament to the legendary mindset's ability to turn challenges into stepping stones for growth.

Sub-Chapter 3.5: Harnessing Inner Strength - The Science of Self-Affirmations

Introduction

Embark on a journey into the realm of self-affirmations, where positive statements transcend mere words and become potent tools for fortifying self-esteem and confidence. In this concise sub-chapter, we unravel the science and practice of self-affirmations, illustrating how they serve as the scaffolding for the legendary mindset.

The Essence of Self-Affirmations

Self-affirmations are not just positive statements; they are the essence of self-empowerment. Delve into the transformative nature of affirming your worth and abilities. Understand how these affirmations act as a shield against self-doubt and as a source of strength that propels you forward on your legendary journey.

Science and Practice Unveiled

Explore the science behind self-affirmations, dissecting how they impact your brain and shape your perception of yourself. Delve into the practical aspects of incorporating affirmations into your daily routine, making them a cornerstone of your mindset. Witness how consistent practice transforms positive affirmations into powerful catalysts for self-esteem and confidence.

Building Resilience Through Affirmations

In the face of challenges, self-affirmations become the bedrock of resilience. Discover how these positive statements fortify your mindset, fostering a belief in your capabilities. Learn to wield affirmations as tools to navigate through adversity, emerging stronger and more resolute on your path to legendary thinking.

Integrating Affirmations into Your Daily Rituals

In this sub-chapter, self-affirmations cease to be mere words; they become integral components of your daily rituals. Uncover practical strategies for seamlessly integrating affirmations into your routine, ensuring that they are not just a practice but a lifestyle. Witness the trans formative power of self-affirmations as they shape the narrative of your legendary journey.

*Resilience
and
adaptability*

CONTENTS

4.1 The Art of Resilience

Explore the intricacies of resilience as an art form in the legendary mindset. Understand how resilience serves as the bedrock of mental fortitude, allowing you to withstand the storms of life and emerge stronger on the other side.

4.2 Bouncing Back from Failure

Failure is not a dead-end but a stepping stone to success. Uncover the strategies and mindset shifts that enable you to bounce back from failure with renewed determination and a greater understanding of your path to greatness.

4.3 Embracing Change

Change is the only constant in life, and legends not only embrace it but thrive within it. Learn the art of embracing change as a catalyst for growth and evolution on your legendary journey.

4.4 Cultivating Adaptability

Adaptability is a skill that transforms challenges into opportunities. Delve into the practical aspects of cultivating adaptability, allowing you to navigate the ever-shifting landscape of life with grace and resilience.

4.5 Learning from Adversity

Adversity is a formidable teacher on the road to legendary thinking. Explore how adversity, when approached with a growth mindset, becomes a source of profound lessons, shaping you into a more resilient and adaptable individual.

Chapter 4: Resilience and Adaptability

Introduction

Resilience and adaptability are the dynamic forces that fortify the legendary mindset, enabling individuals to navigate the complex seas of challenges and changes. In this chapter, we delve into the art of resilience, the ability to bounce back from failure, the embrace of change, the cultivation of adaptability, and the invaluable lessons learned from adversity.

Sub-Chapter 4.1: Mastering The Art of Resilience

Introduction

Unveil the nuanced artistry of resilience within the legendary mindset. In this sub-chapter, we navigate the intricate details of resilience as a masterful creation, solidifying the bedrock of mental fortitude. Explore the transformative power that not only allows you to weather life's storms but propels you to emerge stronger on the other side.

Strategies for Resilience Mastery

Delve into practical strategies that facilitate the mastery of resilience. Understand how legendary individuals navigate challenges with a resilient mindset, turning adversity into a catalyst for personal growth. These strategies act as guiding lights on your journey to becoming a more resilient and empowered individual.

The Resilient Mindset in Action

Witness the resilient mindset in action through real-life examples and anecdotes. This sub-chapter explores how embracing resilience becomes a way of life, influencing decision-making, problem-solving, and overall well-being. The resilient mindset, once cultivated, permeates every aspect of your legendary journey.

Empowering Your Legendary Odyssey

In this exploration of resilience mastery, envision it not just as a skill but as a source of empowerment on your legendary odyssey. As you internalize the art of resilience, it becomes a dynamic force that propels you forward, ensuring that challenges become stepping stones rather than roadblocks.

Cultivating Resilience as a Daily Practice

Discover how resilience can be a daily practice rather than a response to crises. This section provides actionable steps to infuse resilience into your everyday life, creating a resilient mindset that becomes second nature. Embrace resilience as a proactive force, shaping your responses to challenges and fostering personal growth consistently.

Sub-Chapter 4.2: Triumph Over Setbacks

Introduction

Embark on a journey of understanding and triumph over setbacks in the legendary mindset. In this sub-chapter, we unravel the mindset and strategies that empower individuals to not only overcome failure but to use it as a stepping stone on the path to greatness. Discover how setbacks become transformative catalysts for growth in the legendary narrative.

The Mindset Shift: Failure as a Stepping Stone

Explore the profound mindset shift that reframes failure from a stumbling block to a crucial stepping stone. Legendary individuals perceive setbacks as opportunities for learning and improvement. This mindset shift becomes the cornerstone of bouncing back from failure with resilience and determination.

Strategies for Bouncing Back

Delve into practical strategies that facilitate the process of bouncing back from failure. Learn how to extract lessons from setbacks, adapt your approach, and emerge stronger. These strategies are not just survival tools; they are instruments for thriving in the face of adversity.

Learning and Growth Through Failure

Witness how failure, when approached with the right mindset, becomes a dynamic force for learning and growth. This sub-chapter unfolds stories of resilience and triumph, where setbacks are not the end but a necessary chapter in the legendary journey.

Empowering Your Bounce-Back Story

In this exploration, failure isn't a mark of defeat but a narrative of empowerment. Envision how your bounce-back story becomes a testament to your resilience and determination on the path to greatness. Each setback becomes a stepping stone, propelling you forward with newfound strength and insight.

Sub-Chapter 4.3: Embracing Change

Introduction

Within the legendary mindset, change is not a daunting force but a transformative ally. In this sub-chapter, we navigate the art of embracing change as a catalyst for growth and evolution on your extraordinary journey. Discover how legends not only accept change but thrive within its dynamic embrace.

The Dynamic Nature of Change

Understand the inherent nature of change – a constant force that shapes our lives. Legendary individuals recognize change as an opportunity for renewal, growth, and adaptation. Embracing change is not merely a response; it's an intentional strategy for evolving into the best version of oneself.

Navigating the Seas of Transformation

Delve into the practical aspects of embracing change. Learn how to navigate the unpredictable seas of transformation with grace and resilience. Legendary individuals understand that change is not to be feared but harnessed, becoming a powerful force propelling them toward new heights of greatness.

The Growth Catalyst Within Change

Explore how change serves as a catalyst for personal and professional growth. Within the legendary narrative, change is not an obstacle but a stepping stone. Discover the mindset and practices that allow you to not only weather the storms of change but to harness their energy for unparalleled advancement.

Thriving in the Dance of Adaptation

Witness the dance of adaptation as an integral part of embracing change. Legendary individuals don't merely survive change; they thrive within its rhythm. Envision how your legendary journey becomes a testament to the transformative power of embracing change, making every twist and turn a step closer to your aspirations.

Sub-Chapter 4.4 Cultivating Adaptability

Introduction

Adaptability is the secret weapon in the arsenal of the legendary mindset, turning challenges into opportunities. In this sub-chapter, we explore the art of cultivating adaptability, a skill that allows you to navigate the ever-shifting landscape of life with grace and resilience. Witness how legends not only embrace change but dance with it, transforming adversity into triumph.

The Essence of Adaptability

Understand adaptability as a dynamic and essential trait in the legendary journey. Legends cultivate the ability to adjust and thrive in various circumstances. Adaptability is not a reaction; it's a proactive approach to life's uncertainties, a skill that positions you as the master of change rather than its subject.

Practical Strategies for Cultivating Adaptability

Delve into practical strategies for cultivating adaptability in your daily life. Learn how to develop a mindset that views challenges as opportunities for growth. Cultivate the flexibility to adjust your sails in the ever-changing winds of life, ensuring that you not only endure but flourish in the face of challenges.

Adaptability as a Strength, Not a Compromise

Shift your perspective on adaptability from a compromise to a strength. Legendary individuals see adaptability as a strategic advantage, a quality that allows them to navigate the complexities of life with finesse. Explore how cultivating adaptability becomes a transformative force in your legendary journey, propelling you toward unparalleled success.

Thriving Amidst the Winds of Change

Envision yourself not just weathering the winds of change but thriving amidst them. Adaptability is not about surviving; it's about flourishing in the dance of transformation. As you cultivate adaptability, your journey becomes a testament to the strength and resilience that define the legendary mindset.

Sub-Chapter 4.5 Learning from Adversity

Introduction

Adversity, viewed through the lens of the legendary mindset, is not a roadblock but a powerful teacher. In this sub-chapter, we explore how adversity, approached with a growth mindset, becomes a source of profound lessons, shaping you into a more resilient and adaptable individual. Witness how legends turn adversity into a stepping stone for unparalleled progress.

The Role of Adversity in the Legendary Narrative

Understand adversity as an integral part of the legendary narrative. Legends do not shy away from challenges; they confront them with courage and determination. Adversity is not a detour but a vital part of the journey, offering lessons that propel you toward your legendary aspirations.

Extracting Wisdom from Challenges

Delve into the process of extracting wisdom from challenges. Learn how to approach adversity not as a setback but as an opportunity for growth and learning. Legendary individuals transform hardships into stepping stones, extracting valuable insights that contribute to their continuous development.

The Growth Mindset in Adversity

Explore the symbiotic relationship between a growth mindset and adversity. Legends understand that challenges are not obstacles to be avoided but opportunities to be embraced. Witness how adopting a growth mindset in the face of adversity transforms setbacks into catalysts for unparalleled personal and professional growth.

Adversity as a Catalyst for Legendary Progress

Envision adversity not as a barrier but as a catalyst propelling you toward legendary progress. With each challenge confronted and overcome, your journey becomes a testament to the resilience, adaptability, and growth that define the legendary mindset.

Positive thinking
and
Mindfulness

CONTENT

Sub-Chapter 5.1: The Impact of Positive Thinking

Positive thinking isn't just a mindset; it's a force that reverberates through your thoughts, actions, and outcomes. Explore the profound impact of cultivating positivity and understand how it becomes a cornerstone in building your legendary mindset.

Sub-Chapter 5.2: Practicing Gratitude

Gratitude is a transformative practice, a lens through which you view the richness of your life. Delve into the practice of gratitude, discovering how it enhances your perception, cultivates resilience, and becomes a cornerstone of your legendary journey.

Sub-Chapter 5.3: The Science of Happiness

Unravel the science behind happiness and how positive thinking plays a pivotal role. Dive into the principles that govern happiness and learn how aligning your thoughts with positivity contributes to a more fulfilling and legendary life.

Sub-Chapter 5.4: The Mindful Mindset

Mindfulness is more than a practice; it's a way of life. Explore the mindful mindset, understanding how being present in the moment shapes your thoughts, actions, and responses, becoming an integral part of your legendary mindset.

Sub-Chapter 5.5: Meditation and Mindfulness Techniques

Journey into the realm of meditation and mindfulness techniques, discovering practical approaches to integrate these practices into your daily life. Explore the profound impact they have on your mental well-being and their role in nurturing a legendary mindset.

Chapter 5: Mastering the Art of Adaptation

Introduction

Adaptation is the heartbeat of legendary thinking, the ability to embrace change and not just survive, but thrive in the face of uncertainty. It's the art of evolving with grace, learning from life's inevitable curveballs, and seizing the reins of your destiny in ever-changing landscapes. In this chapter, we delve into how legendary individuals master the art of adaptation, utilizing it as a powerful tool for continuous growth and personal evolution.

Sub-Chapter 5.1 Embracing Change as an Opportunity

Introduction

Change is the constant in life's ever-shifting narrative. Legendary thinkers do not fear it; they greet it with open arms, for they recognize change as an opportunity for self-reinvention. They embrace change as a chance to embark on new adventures, explore uncharted territories, and redefine what's possible.

Navigating the Winds of Change

Legendary individuals navigate the winds of change with purpose and poise. This section explores the mindset and strategies that allow them to not only weather the storms of change but to harness its winds, propelling them toward new horizons. Discover the art of embracing change as a transformative force in the legendary journey.

Change as a Catalyst for Personal Evolution

In the hands of a legendary thinker, change becomes a catalyst for personal evolution. Learn how embracing change facilitates continuous growth, enabling individuals to shed old skins and emerge stronger, wiser, and more resilient. Understand the role of change in shaping a legendary mindset.

The Dance of Innovation in Changing Landscapes

Change invites the dance of innovation, and legends are the choreographers of this transformative ballet. Explore how embracing change sparks innovation, allowing individuals to push boundaries, challenge norms, and usher in positive transformations in their lives and the world around them.

The Ripple Effect of Change in Personal Growth

Change not only reshapes external landscapes but also catalyzes internal transformations. This part delves into how legendary individuals harness the ripple effect of change to foster personal growth, creativity, and adaptability. Witness the profound impact of embracing change on the mindset of a legendary thinker.

Sub-Chapter 5.2 The Agile Mindset

Introduction

An agile mindset is a flexible and adaptable perspective on life. It's the capacity to pivot, recalibrate, and respond to shifting circumstances with fluid grace. Legends cultivate an agile mindset, allowing them to navigate the unpredictable waters of existence with the poise of a seasoned sailor.

Flexibility as a Superpower

Legendary individuals view flexibility as a superpower in the face of life's uncertainties. This section explores how an agile mindset enables them to adapt swiftly to changing situations, making them resilient in the midst of challenges. Discover the strategies that transform flexibility into a cornerstone of the legendary journey.

Recalibrating in the Face of Change

The ability to recalibrate is a hallmark of the agile mindset. Delve into the art of recalibration as legends share their strategies for realigning goals, priorities, and perspectives in response to evolving circumstances. Witness how recalibrating becomes a strategic move in the game of legendary thinking.

Responding to Life's Curveballs

Life's curveballs are inevitable, but legends are adept at hitting them out of the park. Explore how an agile mindset equips individuals to respond skillfully to unexpected challenges, turning potential setbacks into opportunities for growth. Learn the invaluable skill of staying nimble in the face of adversity.

Adaptability as a Continuous Practice

Adopting an agile mindset is not a one-time event but a continuous practice. Understand how legendary thinkers integrate adaptability into their daily lives, making it a natural and instinctive part of their approach to challenges. Witness the transformative power of an agile mindset in the legendary journey.

Navigating the Ebb and Flow of Change

The agile mindset is not just about reacting to change but also about navigating its ebb and flow. This part explores how legends skillfully ride the waves of change, using its momentum to propel themselves forward. Gain insights into the art of gracefully navigating life's ever-changing currents.

Sub-Chapter 5.4 The Power of Resilience in Adaptation

Introduction

Resilience is the bedrock upon which adaptation thrives. When faced with change and challenges, resilient individuals do not crumble; they bend and adapt. Resilience empowers them to weather storms and come out the other side even more robust and resolute.

Building Resilience as a Skill

This section explores resilience not as an inherent trait but as a skill that can be honed and strengthened. Delve into the practices and mindset shifts that contribute to building resilience. Learn how cultivating resilience becomes a transformative process, preparing you to navigate the unpredictable twists of life with unwavering strength.

Navigating Change with Resilience

Change is inevitable, but with resilience, it becomes an opportunity rather than a threat. Discover how legends navigate through the uncertainties of life with resilience as their compass. Gain insights into the practical strategies that resilient individuals employ when faced with change, turning potential disruptions into stepping stones for growth.

Resilience as a Source of Inner Strength

Resilience is not merely about bouncing back; it's about discovering an inner strength that withstands the tests of time. Explore how building resilience becomes a journey of self-discovery, unveiling reservoirs of strength and courage you never knew existed. Witness how this inner resilience becomes the bedrock of your legendary journey.

The Role of Mindset in Resilience

Your mindset shapes your response to challenges, and resilience is closely tied to your mental outlook. This part delves into the role of mindset in resilience, exploring how adopting a growth-oriented perspective enhances your ability to adapt and thrive. Uncover the transformative power of cultivating a resilient mindset.

Resilience as a Catalyst for Growth

For legendary thinkers, resilience is not just a defensive mechanism; it's a catalyst for growth. This section explores how resilience propels individuals forward, enabling them to turn challenges into opportunities for personal and professional advancement. Gain insights into how resilience becomes the cornerstone for creating a legendary legacy.

Sub-Chapter 5.5 The Role of Curiosity and Innovation

Introduction

Curiosity and innovation are the twin engines of adaptation. Legendary individuals are not satisfied with the status quo; they are driven by a deep sense of curiosity, an insatiable thirst for knowledge, and an unyielding desire to innovate. They view adaptation as an opportunity to explore new possibilities, challenge the conventional, and create positive change in the world.

Curiosity as the Spark of Adaptation

In this section, we delve into the role of curiosity as the spark that ignites the flame of adaptation. Understand how curiosity propels legendary thinkers to ask questions, seek new perspectives, and constantly explore the boundaries of their understanding. Witness how curiosity becomes the driving force that fuels the continuous quest for growth and adaptation.

The Innovative Mindset

Innovation is not just about groundbreaking discoveries; it's a mindset that embraces change and leverages creativity to solve challenges. Explore how legends cultivate an innovative mindset, approaching problems with a fresh perspective and seeing opportunities where others see obstacles. Learn how this mindset becomes a beacon guiding them through the ever-evolving landscape of life.

Creating Positive Change Through Innovation

For legendary individuals, innovation is not just a personal trait; it's a tool for creating positive change in the world. This part explores how curiosity and innovation combine to drive individuals towards making a meaningful impact on their communities and beyond. Witness how legendary thinkers use their innovative spirit to leave a lasting legacy of progress and transformation.

Adapting to the Future Through Curiosity and Innovation

The future is uncertain, but legendary thinkers approach it with anticipation rather than fear. This section examines how curiosity and innovation act as compasses, guiding individuals through the uncharted territories of the future. Gain insights into how cultivating these qualities enables legends to adapt, thrive, and lead in a world of constant change.

Harnessing the Power of Curiosity and Innovation

In conclusion, this part explores the overarching theme of how curiosity and innovation collectively harness their power. Discover how, as a legendary thinker, you can leverage the dynamic interplay between curiosity and innovation to not only adapt to change but also actively shape the future. Explore the transformative potential of combining curiosity with innovative thinking on your legendary journey.

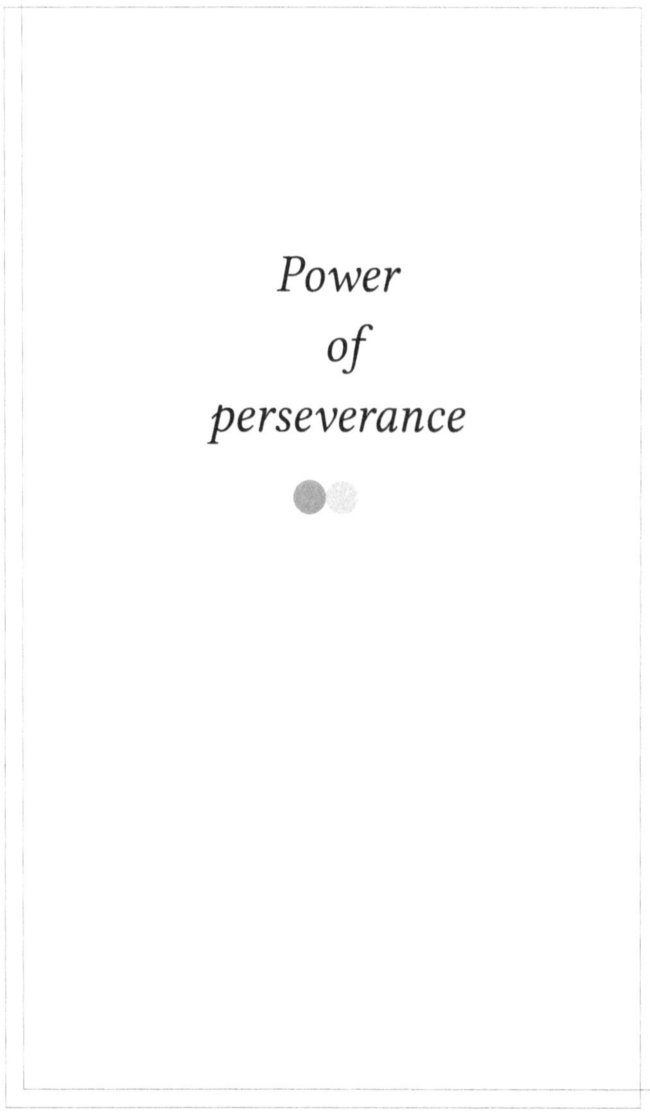

*Power
of
perseverance*

CONTENTS

Chapter 6: The Power of Perseverance

Introduction

Within the tapestry of legendary thinking, perseverance emerges as the unwavering force propelling individuals through challenges, setbacks, and triumphs. In this expansive chapter, we navigate through the transformative power embedded in perseverance. We unravel the stories of legendary figures, explore the profound significance of never yielding, resist the allure of instant gratification, delve into the interplay between passion and persistence, and unlock the secrets to maintaining unwavering motivation.

Sub-Chapter 6.1 The Story of Legends

Story of legends

Embark on a mythic journey through the annals of legendary tales, where ordinary individuals transcended the realms of possibility to become icons of greatness. Discover the story of legends, born not from divine origins but forged in the crucible of relentless perseverance.

Anti-Apartheid Activism:

Nelson Mandela's legendary journey began with his tireless activism against apartheid in South Africa. Despite facing imprisonment and enduring harsh conditions on Robben Island, Mandela remained unwavering in his pursuit of justice, becoming a symbol of resistance against racial oppression.

Imprisonment and Resilience:

Mandela's 27-year imprisonment could have broken a lesser spirit, but he transformed adversity into strength. His resilience during those challenging years not only sustained him but fueled a global movement calling for his release. Mandela emerged from prison with a spirit unbroken and a commitment to reconciliation.

Presidency and Reconciliation:

Mandela's presidency marked a transformative era for South Africa. Instead of seeking revenge, he advocated for reconciliation and forgiveness, steering the nation away from the brink of racial conflict. Mandela's leadership exemplifies the power of forgiveness and unity in building a more just and inclusive society.

presidency marked a transformative era for South Africa. Instead of seeking revenge, he advocated for reconciliation and forgiveness, steering the nation away from the brink of racial conflict. Mandela's leadership exemplifies the power of forgiveness and unity in building a more just and inclusive society.

Explore the iMandela'sntricacies of resilience as an art form in the legendary mindset. Understand how the tales of legends serve as a foundational cornerstone, illuminating the path to greatness and offering a roadmap for those who dare to dream beyond conventional boundaries.

In the heart of this narrative, witness the struggles and triumphs of those who faced adversity with unwavering determination. Their stories illuminate the path to greatness, offering a roadmap for those who dare to dream beyond conventional boundaries.

Learn that legends are not distant deities but mortals who embraced challenges, navigated setbacks, and transformed failures into stepping stones toward their ambitions. Understand that the essence of legendary thinking lies not in the absence of challenges but in the indomitable spirit to rise above them.

As you traverse the mythic landscape of these tales, recognize that the same potential resides within you. You, too, can script your legend by embracing the ethos of perseverance, refusing to yield to the allure of instant gratification, and turning challenges into catalysts for growth.

In the story of legends, find the inspiration to carve your narrative of greatness. The tapestry of your journey awaits the threads of resilience, passion, and an unwavering spirit. Become the protagonist of your myth, for in the realm of possibility, you are the architect of your own legendary saga.

Sub-Chapter 6.2 The Unyielding Spirit

Introduction

The unyielding spirit is the anchor of legendary perseverance, embodying the refusal to surrender in the face of challenges. In this section, we unravel the essence of an unyielding spirit, exploring the principles and strategies that elevate ordinary individuals to the realm of legends.

Forged in the Crucible of Challenges

Legendary individuals are not born with an unyielding spirit; they forge it in the crucible of challenges. Delve into the transformative experiences that shape an unyielding mindset. Understand how facing adversity head-on becomes the catalyst for building an indomitable spirit.

Mindset Shifts for Unwavering Resolve

Explore the mindset shifts that differentiate an unyielding spirit from mere persistence. Legends cultivate mental habits that foster unwavering resolve, allowing them to navigate hardships with tenacity. Learn how to adopt these mindset shifts and apply them to your own journey toward legendary thinking.

Turning Setbacks into Springboards

In the legendary mindset, setbacks are not setbacks; they are springboards for growth. This part explores the art of reframing setbacks, transforming them from stumbling blocks into stepping stones. Gain insights into how legends leverage setbacks as opportunities to propel themselves toward greater heights.

Rising Strong: Resilience in Action

Resilience is the heartbeat of an unyielding spirit. Legendary individuals don't just bounce back; they rise stronger from every fall. Explore how resilience manifests in real-life situations, providing the strength to endure and the courage to persevere. Witness resilience as the force that defines a truly unyielding spirit.

Cultivating a Legendary Resolve

Cultivating an unyielding spirit goes beyond facing challenges; it involves nurturing a legendary resolve. This section delves into the daily practices and habits that sustain an unyielding mindset. Discover how consistency and commitment become the pillars of a legendary individual's enduring spirit.

Sub-Chapter 6.3 Resisting Instant Gratification

Introduction

In a world driven by instant results, resisting the allure of immediate rewards is a hallmark of the legendary mindset. This section delves into the inherent value of delayed gratification, unraveling how this ability becomes the bedrock of perseverance on the challenging path to enduring success.

The Strategic Art of Patience

Legendary individuals understand that patience is not passive waiting but a strategic choice. Explore the strategic art of patience and delayed gratification as powerful tools in the arsenal of perseverance. Learn how to navigate the tension between short-term temptations and long-term goals with poise and determination.

Investing in Long-Term Excellence

Uncover the importance of investing in long-term goals over succumbing to the temptation of instant gratification. Legendary thinkers view success as a journey, not a destination, and understand that enduring excellence requires the discipline to withstand the allure of quick rewards. Discover how this mindset fosters perseverance in the pursuit of greatness.

Turning Challenges into Opportunities

In the realm of legendary thinking, challenges are not obstacles but opportunities for growth. This part explores how resisting instant gratification turns challenges into strategic opportunities. Gain insights into how legends leverage the discipline of delayed gratification to transform obstacles into stepping stones on their path to enduring success.

Sustainable Success Through Patience

Success that stands the test of time is built on the foundation of patience and delayed gratification. Explore how sustainable success becomes the natural byproduct of a mindset that values enduring excellence over fleeting pleasures. Learn how to integrate the principles of patience into your journey, ensuring your success is not just immediate but enduring.

Sub-Chapter 6.4 Passion and Persistence

Introduction

Passion and persistence are the dynamic duo driving the legendary mindset, propelling individuals forward on their epic odyssey. This section delves into the intricate dance between profound passion and unwavering persistence, unraveling how these forces synergize to forge an unbreakable spirit on the path to greatness.

The Flame of Profound Passion

At the heart of legendary perseverance lies a flame of profound passion. Explore how passion serves as the catalyst that ignites the fires within, transforming challenges into opportunities for expression and growth. Learn the art of identifying and nurturing your passion, turning it into the driving force behind your every endeavor.

The Symbiotic Relationship with Persistence

Passion finds its true partner in persistence. Witness the symbiotic relationship between passion and persistence, understanding how one reinforces and amplifies the other. Delve into the mindset and strategies that enable individuals to persist in the face of adversity, making every step forward a testament to their enduring commitment.

Overcoming Obstacles with Passion

Obstacles are inevitable on the journey to greatness, but passion becomes the compass that guides individuals through the darkest moments. Explore how legends overcome obstacles with an unwavering passion, turning challenges into stepping stones and setbacks into opportunities for deeper self-discovery.

Passion as a Source of Renewed Energy

In the face of fatigue and challenges, passion becomes the wellspring of renewed energy. This part explores how passion revitalizes individuals, allowing them to recharge and persevere with a heightened sense of purpose. Learn the art of tapping into your passion as a constant source of motivation and resilience.

Fostering a Culture of Passion

Legends not only embody passion but also cultivate it in their environments. Discover how to foster a culture of passion within your personal and professional spheres. Explore the ripple effect of passion, inspiring not only yourself but also those around you to embrace the transformative power of unwavering commitment.

Sub-Chapter 6.5 Staying Motivated

Introduction

Sustained motivation is the lifeblood of the legendary mindset, fueling the relentless pursuit of greatness through the inevitable highs and lows. This section unravels the secrets behind the unwavering motivation that propels legends to maintain focus, overcome burnout, and reignite the flame of determination on their extraordinary journey.

Cultivating Intrinsic Motivation

Legendary individuals don't merely rely on external factors for motivation; they cultivate intrinsic motivation from within. Explore the art of tapping into your inner drive, aligning your goals with your values, and fostering a deep sense of purpose. Learn how intrinsic motivation becomes a sustainable force that propels you forward even when external circumstances waver.

Navigating Burnout with Grace

Burnout is a common challenge on the road to greatness, but legends understand how to navigate it with grace. Delve into strategies for recognizing and addressing burnout, ensuring that challenges don't derail your motivation. Learn the art of self-care, resilience, and maintaining a healthy balance to sustain your passion.

Harnessing Setbacks as Motivational Fuel

In the legendary journey, setbacks aren't deterrents; they are sources of motivational fuel. Explore how legends use setbacks as catalysts to reignite their determination. Gain insights into turning adversity into motivation, transforming challenges into stepping stones that propel you forward with renewed vigor.

Creating a Motivational Ecosystem

Legendary thinkers create a holistic ecosystem that nurtures motivation. This part explores how your environment, habits, and support systems play a crucial role in sustaining motivation. Learn to build a motivational ecosystem that reinforces your commitment, empowers your resilience, and ensures your journey remains fueled by an unyielding determination.

Evolving Motivation with Evolving Goals

As your journey unfolds, so do your goals. Legends understand the importance of evolving motivation in tandem with evolving objectives. Explore how to adapt and recalibrate your motivation to align with changing circumstances, ensuring a dynamic and responsive approach to the pursuit of enduring greatness.

building meaningful relationships

CONTENTS

Chapter 7: Building Meaningful Relationships

Introduction

Embark on a journey of connection within the legendary mindset with Chapter 7, where the tapestry of your legendary existence is woven through meaningful relationships. Building a network of support, mastering effective communication, fostering empathy and connection, handling conflict with grace, and embracing collaboration and teamwork are the pillars that form the infrastructure of your legendary social landscape.

Sub-Chapter 7.1: Building a Supportive Network

Introduction

Embark on a journey to build a supportive network within the legendary mindset. Like the sturdy branches of a mighty tree, a supportive network provides strength and stability on your path to greatness. In this section, we delve into the art of cultivating relationships that uplift and empower, creating a foundation of support as you navigate the challenges of your legendary journey.

The Roots of Supportive Relationships

Just as a tree draws strength from its roots, your journey to greatness is fortified by the depth of your relationships. Explore the foundational principles that underpin supportive connections, understanding the importance of trust, mutual respect, and shared values in cultivating a network that stands the test of time.

Nurturing Growth Through Connections

A supportive network is not static; it evolves and grows with intention. Learn how to nurture the growth of your relationships, fostering an environment where each individual contributes to the collective strength of the network. Discover the reciprocity inherent in supportive connections, where the growth of one becomes the growth of all.

Empowering Each Branch

In a supportive network, each individual is like a branch, contributing to the overall strength of the collective. Delve into strategies that empower each member of your network, recognizing and leveraging the unique strengths and qualities they bring. Understand how the synergy of empowered individuals creates a resilient and robust support system.

The Network as a Lifeline

In times of challenge and triumph, your supportive network serves as a lifeline. Explore how to lean on and contribute to this lifeline, fostering a culture of support that weaves through the fabric of your legendary journey. Understand the reciprocity of support, where giving and receiving create a dynamic equilibrium that propels everyone forward.

This section invites you to build and sustain a supportive network that not only provides strength and stability but also amplifies the collective impact of each individual on the legendary path.

Sub-Chapter 7.2: Effective Communication

Introduction

Embark on a transformative exploration of effective communication within the legendary mindset. Communication is not merely the exchange of words; it's the bridge that connects minds and hearts. In this section, we unravel the nuances of effective communication, delving into the art of expressing yourself authentically and fostering meaningful connections in both personal and professional realms.

The Essence of Authentic Expression

Effective communication begins with authenticity. Discover the power of expressing your thoughts, feelings, and intentions with sincerity and clarity. Uncover the nuances of authenticity, understanding how genuine communication forms the bedrock of deep and meaningful connections within your network.

Active Listening as a Gateway

Communication is a two-way street, and active listening is the gateway to understanding. Explore the art of listening with intention and presence, cultivating the ability to truly hear and comprehend the perspectives of others. Learn how active listening enriches your relationships and contributes to a culture of mutual understanding.

Non-Verbal Language and Presence

Communication extends beyond words to encompass non-verbal cues and presence. Delve into the intricacies of body language, facial expressions, and overall presence, understanding how these elements convey messages that can either enhance or detract from the effectiveness of your communication. Explore the art of aligning your non-verbal language with your authentic expression.

Navigating Communication Challenges

In the vast landscape of communication, challenges may arise. Explore strategies for navigating communication challenges with grace and resilience. Whether faced with misunderstandings, conflicts, or differing perspectives, learn how to approach these challenges as opportunities for growth and strengthened connections.

Empowering Your Network Through Communication

Effective communication empowers not only individuals but the entire network. Discover how your communication style can contribute to the empowerment of others, fostering an environment where every voice is heard and valued. Understand the ripple effect of empowering communication on the collective strength of your supportive network.

This section invites you to hone your communication skills, recognizing them as essential tools for fostering understanding, connection, and empowerment within your network on the legendary journey.

Sub-Chapter 7.3: Empathy and Connection

Introduction

Embark on a profound exploration of empathy and connection within the legendary mindset. In the tapestry of meaningful relationships, empathy is the golden thread that weaves a fabric of understanding and compassion. This section delves into the transformative power of empathy, inviting you to forge connections that transcend surface interactions and stand the test of time.

Understanding the Essence of Empathy

Empathy is the ability to understand and share the feelings of another. Explore the essence of empathy, delving into the nuances of recognizing, acknowledging, and resonating with the emotions of those around you. Understand how cultivating empathy deepens your connections and contributes to the richness of your network.

Building Bridges of Understanding

Empathy serves as a bridge that connects hearts and minds. Learn how to build these bridges of understanding through empathetic communication. Explore strategies for tuning into the experiences and perspectives of others, fostering an environment where everyone feels seen, heard, and valued.

Cultivating a Culture of Empathy

Within a supportive network, empathy cultivates a culture of compassion and support. Delve into the dynamics of creating a culture where empathy thrives, contributing to an atmosphere of trust, collaboration, and genuine care. Understand the ripple effect of empathy on the overall strength and resilience of your relationships.

Navigating Empathy Challenges

While empathy is a powerful force, challenges may arise. Explore strategies for navigating empathy challenges, such as understanding boundaries and avoiding emotional exhaustion. Learn how to balance empathy with self-care, ensuring that your capacity for understanding and connection remains sustainable.

The

Enduring Bonds of True Connection

True connection goes beyond mere interaction; it is a shared experience of empathy and understanding. Explore how cultivating empathy leads to enduring bonds within your network. Witness the transformation of relationships when rooted in the deep soil of genuine connection, creating a network that flourishes and stands resilient against the winds of change.

This section invites you to embrace empathy as a cornerstone of your legendary relationships, recognizing its transformative power in fostering deep, meaningful, and enduring connections within your supportive network.

Sub-Chapter 7.4: Handling Conflict

Introduction

Within the intricate tapestry of relationships, conflict emerges as a natural thread, capable of either unraveling connections or weaving them tighter. In this section, we delve into the art of handling conflict within the legendary mindset. Here, conflict is not viewed as a detriment but as an opportunity for growth, understanding, and the strengthening of bonds.

Reframing Conflict as an Opportunity

Conflict is a natural part of any relationship, yet its perception can be transformed. Explore the mindset shift that reframes conflict as an opportunity for growth. Understand how conflicts, when navigated with poise and wisdom, can lead to deeper understanding, resilience, and an enhanced capacity for collaboration.

Communication Strategies for Conflict Resolution

Effective communication becomes the compass in the midst of conflict. Delve into communication strategies that foster resolution, understanding, and compromise. Explore the power of active listening, assertiveness, and empathy in navigating conflicts, transforming them from adversarial encounters to collaborative discussions.

Navigating Emotional Responses

Emotions often run high during conflicts, and navigating them is a crucial skill. Explore techniques for managing and understanding emotional responses, both yours and others'. Understand the role of emotional intelligence in conflict resolution and how it contributes to creating an environment of mutual respect.

Collaborative Problem-Solving

Conflicts present an opportunity for collaborative problem-solving. Learn how to approach conflicts as challenges to be solved together, fostering a sense of shared responsibility. Explore techniques for finding common ground, identifying mutual goals, and collectively working toward resolutions that benefit all parties involved.

Mediation and Seeking Professional Help

In certain instances, conflicts may benefit from external intervention. Explore the option of mediation and seeking professional help when conflicts become entrenched. Understand how unbiased facilitation can provide new perspectives and guide the resolution process toward a mutually agreeable outcome.

The Transformative Power of Conflict Resolution

Handled with grace and intention, conflict resolution becomes a transformative force. Explore how successfully navigating conflicts contributes to the strength and resilience of relationships. Witness the evolution of connections when conflicts are not avoided but approached with a commitment to understanding and growth.

This section invites you to master the art of conflict resolution within the legendary mindset, recognizing conflicts not as obstacles but as opportunities to deepen connections and fortify the bonds within your supportive network.

Sub-Chapter 7.5: Collaboration and Teamwork

Introduction

In this concluding section of Chapter 7, we explore the transformative power of working in unison with others. Here, collaboration is not merely a strategy but a mindset, and teamwork becomes the driving force behind achieving feats beyond individual capabilities.

Fostering a Collaborative Mindset

Collaboration begins with a mindset that values collective success. Delve into the foundational aspects of fostering a collaborative mindset, where the achievements of the group are cherished as much as individual accomplishments. Understand how this mindset sets the stage for effective teamwork and shared success.

Effective Communication in Teams

Communication forms the backbone of successful collaboration. Explore the dynamics of effective communication within teams, from clear articulation of ideas to active listening. Understand how transparent and open communication fosters an environment where diverse perspectives are welcomed and collaboration flourishes.

Building Synergy in Team Dynamics

Synergy is the magic that occurs when individuals work together seamlessly. Explore the elements that contribute to building synergy in team dynamics. Understand how complementary strengths, shared goals, and a sense of camaraderie create a collective energy that propels the team toward extraordinary achievements.

Navigating Challenges in Team Settings

Teamwork isn't without its challenges, but legends understand how to navigate them with grace. Delve into strategies for handling challenges within a team setting, from resolving conflicts to addressing differing opinions. Learn how challenges, when approached collaboratively, become stepping stones toward greater cohesion.

Recognizing and Valuing Contributions

Every team member is a crucial note in the symphony of collaboration. Explore the importance of recognizing and valuing each member's contributions. Understand how acknowledging individual strengths and celebrating achievements fosters a sense of belonging and encourages sustained collaboration.

Strategic Planning and Goal Alignment

Effective collaboration is guided by strategic planning and aligned goals. Explore how legends approach collaborative endeavors with a clear roadmap, ensuring that each team member understands their role in achieving collective objectives. Learn the art of aligning individual goals with the overarching vision of the team.

Celebrating Collective Success

In the culmination of collaborative efforts lies the celebration of collective success. Explore the significance of acknowledging and celebrating milestones achieved through teamwork. Understand how shared victories not only strengthen the bonds within the team but also contribute to the overall narrative of legendary thinking.

As we conclude this exploration into the realm of collaboration and teamwork, envision these principles as the pillars supporting your journey. In the chapters to come, we will continue to unravel the layers of the legendary mindset, guiding you toward greater insights and transformative thinking.

Leadership
and
Influence

CONTENTS

Chapter 8: Leadership and Influence

Introduction

Step into the realm of leadership and influence with Chapter 8, where the essence of legendary thinking takes the form of inspiring leadership. Within this chapter, we explore the qualities that define legendary leaders, the transformative impact of leading by example, the artistry of inspiring others, the nuances of persuasion, and the enduring legacy crafted by those who embrace leadership with a legendary mindset

Sub-Chapter 8.1: The Qualities of Legendary Leaders

Introduction

Embark on a profound exploration of the qualities that define legendary leaders within the legendary mindset. Much like the branches of a mighty tree, these leaders possess a unique set of qualities that set them apart. In this section, we delve into the intricacies of visionary thinking, integrity, resilience, and empathy, understanding how these qualities converge to create leaders who inspire, guide, and propel their teams toward greatness.

Visionary Thinking: Beyond the Horizon

Legendary leaders are visionaries, able to see beyond the immediate and envision a future of possibilities. Explore the nuances of visionary thinking, understanding how the ability to articulate a compelling vision becomes a rallying point for teams. Witness how visionary leaders inspire collective action toward shared goals.

Integrity: The Bedrock of Trust

At the core of legendary leadership lies integrity, the unwavering commitment to ethical principles and honesty. Delve into the significance of integrity in leadership, understanding how trust is built and sustained through transparent actions and principled decision-making. Explore the role of integrity in fostering a culture of accountability and credibility.

Resilience: Weathering the Storms

Leadership is not without challenges, and resilience is the cornerstone that enables leaders to weather the storms. Explore the intricacies of resilience in leadership, witnessing how legendary leaders navigate setbacks with grace and emerge stronger. Understand the role of resilience in cultivating a mindset of continuous improvement and adaptability.

Empathy: The Heartbeat of Connection

Empathy is the heartbeat that connects legendary leaders with their teams. Delve into the transformative power of empathy, understanding how the ability to relate to others on a human level fosters trust, collaboration, and a positive organizational culture. Explore how empathetic leaders create environments where individuals feel seen, heard, and valued.

Collaboration: Orchestrating Collective Success

Legendary leaders understand that true success is collective. Explore the nuances of collaboration in leadership, witnessing how effective leaders cultivate a culture of teamwork and shared success. Understand how collaborative leadership harnesses the diverse strengths of a team, propelling the entire organization toward greatness.

This section invites you to explore the qualities that define legendary leaders, recognizing them not as traits of authority but as guiding principles that inspire, connect, and lead teams toward collective success.

Sub-Chapter 8.2: Leading by Example

Introduction

Embark on a transformative journey through the essence of leadership in this exploration of "Leading by Example" within the legendary mindset. Leadership, as an art, extends beyond mere words and finds its profound definition in actions. In this section, we delve into the concept of leading by example, where a leader's behavior and work ethic become a guiding light, illuminating the path for others.

Authenticity and Integrity as Catalysts

At the heart of leading by example lies authenticity and integrity. Explore the transformative power of authentic leadership, understanding how genuine actions resonate with sincerity and establish the foundation for a culture of excellence within a team. Witness how leaders, by embodying integrity in their actions, inspire trust and foster an environment of accountability.

The Illuminating Effect on Team Dynamics

Leadership is a beacon that influences not only individual actions but the collective dynamics of a team. Delve into the illuminating effect of leading by example on team dynamics, witnessing how a leader's commitment to excellence sets a standard for others to follow. Understand how the authenticity of a leader becomes a catalyst for a positive and productive work culture.

Setting Standards for Excellence

In the realm of leadership, actions speak louder than words. Explore how leaders, through their example, set high standards for excellence, challenging their teams to strive for greatness. Witness how a commitment to continuous improvement and dedication to quality work becomes contagious, elevating the overall performance of the entire team.

Cultivating a Culture of Excellence

Leading by example is not just a leadership style; it's a culture. Delve into the nuances of cultivating a culture of excellence within a team, understanding how a leader's actions contribute to a positive and forward-thinking work environment. Explore the ripple effect of this culture on individual growth, collaboration, and overall team success.

This section invites you to explore the essence of leadership through the art of leading by example, recognizing it as a transformative force that shapes team dynamics, sets standards for excellence, and cultivates a culture of continuous improvement within the legendary mindset.

Sub-Chapter 8.3 Inspiring Others

Introduction

Embark on an exploration of the profound role of inspiration within the legendary mindset in this section titled "Inspiring Others." For legendary leaders, inspiration is not just a fleeting moment; it's the currency that fuels the journey of greatness. Delve into the art of inspiring others, tapping into the collective passion and potential of a team.

Fostering a Shared Vision

At the heart of inspiration lies a shared vision that resonates with each team member. Explore how legendary leaders foster a shared vision, aligning individual aspirations with overarching goals. Understand the power of a compelling vision in uniting diverse talents toward a common purpose, creating a sense of purpose and direction.

Nurturing a Positive and Motivating Environment

Inspiration thrives in an environment infused with positivity and motivation. Delve into the art of creating a workplace culture where positivity is not just a buzzword but a lived experience. Witness how legendary leaders nurture an environment that encourages innovation, risk-taking, and the pursuit of excellence.

Igniting the Spark of Passion

Passion is the driving force behind inspired actions. Explore how legendary leaders ignite the spark of passion within their teams, cultivating an atmosphere where individuals are not just employees but contributors to a shared mission. Understand the transformative impact of passion on creativity, productivity, and the overall well-being of the team.

Empowering Through Inspirational Leadership

Inspiration is a form of empowerment. Delve into the ways in which inspirational leadership empowers team members to unlock their full potential. Explore the ripple effect of inspiration on individual and collective performance, fostering an environment where each member feels valued and motivated to contribute their best.

This section invites you to unravel the art of inspiring others, recognizing it as a cornerstone of legendary leadership that goes beyond motivation, shaping a culture where inspiration becomes the driving force behind extraordinary achievements

Sub-Chapter 8.4 The Art of Persuasion

Introduction

Embark on a strategic exploration of the art of persuasion within the legendary mindset in this section titled "The Art of Persuasion." Legendary leaders understand that persuasion is not about manipulation but about effective communication, empathy, and strategic influence. Delve into the nuances of persuasion, understanding how it contributes to a leader's ability to garner support, build consensus, and guide teams toward shared objectives.

Effective Communication as the Foundation

At the core of persuasion lies effective communication. Explore how legendary leaders master the art of conveying their ideas with clarity, conviction, and authenticity. Understand the importance of aligning communication with the values and vision of the team, creating a persuasive narrative that resonates with each team member.

Empathy as a Persuasive Tool

Persuasion is deeply intertwined with empathy. Delve into the role of empathy in understanding the perspectives and needs of others. Explore how legendary leaders leverage empathy as a persuasive tool, creating connections and building trust that form the basis for influential leadership.

Strategic Influence in Decision-Making

In the realm of leadership, decision-making is a pivotal arena for persuasion. Explore how legendary leaders strategically influence decision-making processes, presenting compelling arguments and insights that guide teams toward optimal outcomes. Understand the delicate balance between influence and collaboration in the pursuit of shared goals.

Building Consensus Through Collaboration

Persuasion in leadership is not about unilateral decisions but about building consensus through collaboration. Delve into the collaborative aspects of persuasive leadership, understanding how legendary leaders foster an environment where diverse opinions are valued, and decisions are reached through a collective and informed process.

Ethical Considerations in Persuasive Leadership

Legendary leaders recognize the ethical dimensions of persuasion. Explore how ethical considerations guide persuasive leadership, ensuring that influence is wielded responsibly and in alignment with the values of integrity, transparency, and fairness. Understand the long-term impact of ethical persuasion on trust and team cohesion.

This section invites you to master the art of persuasion within the legendary mindset, recognizing it as a skill that goes beyond mere convincing, fostering collaboration, and guiding teams toward collective success.

Sub-Chapter 8.5 Leaving a Lasting Legacy

Introduction

Embark on a reflective journey into the profound concept of leaving a lasting legacy within the legendary mindset in this section titled "Leaving a Lasting Legacy." Legendary leaders understand that their impact extends beyond their immediate tenure. Delve into the exploration of how leaders can create a positive and enduring legacy on their teams, organizations, and the world at large.

Mentorship as a Catalyst for Growth

Mentorship is a cornerstone of leaving a lasting legacy. Explore how legendary leaders engage in mentorship, guiding and nurturing the next generation of leaders. Understand the transformative impact of mentorship on individual growth, skill development, and the perpetuation of a culture of excellence.

Institutional Impact Through Visionary Leadership

Legendary leaders leave an indelible mark on institutions through visionary leadership. Delve into how leaders can shape the trajectory of organizations, infusing them with values, purpose, and a forward-thinking mindset. Explore the strategic decisions and initiatives that contribute to institutional impact and sustained success.

Creating a Positive Work Culture

A positive work culture is a legacy that transcends time. Explore how legendary leaders cultivate a positive and inclusive work culture, fostering an environment where individuals thrive both personally and professionally. Understand the role of culture in attracting top talent, retaining employees, and ensuring the longevity of the positive legacy.

Innovation and Creativity as Legacy-Building Tools

Legacy-building involves pushing the boundaries of innovation and creativity. Delve into how legendary leaders inspire innovation and creativity within their teams, leaving behind a legacy of forward-thinking solutions and groundbreaking achievements. Explore how a culture of innovation contributes to an organization's resilience and long-term relevance.

Social and Environmental Contributions

Legendary leaders recognize the responsibility to contribute positively to society and the environment. Explore how leaders can leave a legacy by championing social and environmental causes, aligning organizational values with a commitment to making a meaningful difference. Understand the far-reaching impact of such contributions on the reputation and legacy of the leader and the organization.

This section invites you to reflect on the multifaceted nature of leaving a lasting legacy, recognizing it as a purposeful and intentional act within the legendary mindset. Explore the various facets of legacy-building, from mentorship and institutional impact to creating positive work cultures and contributing to social and environmental well-being.

Leadership and Influence

CONTENTS

Chapter 9: Sustaining the Legendary Mindset

Introduction

Embark on an enriching odyssey into the sustaining realms of the legendary mindset with Chapter 9. This chapter unfolds as a vibrant tapestry, weaving together the principles that uphold the very fabric of your legendary existence. Explore the nuances of continual growth, the enduring essence of success, the delicate dance between life and triumph, the art of legacy, and the perpetual journey that defines a true legend.

Sub-Chapter 9.1 Continual Growth and Learning

Introduction

Embark on a transformative exploration of continual growth and learning within the legendary mindset in this section titled "Continual Growth and Learning." For legendary individuals, the journey of greatness is an unending quest for knowledge, improvement, and evolution. Delve into the commitment to lifelong learning, understanding how it forms the bedrock of sustained success and the legendary mindset.

The Pursuit of Knowledge as a Lifestyle

Knowledge is not a destination but a lifelong companion on the legendary journey. Explore how legendary individuals cultivate a mindset that embraces continual learning as a lifestyle. Understand the role of curiosity, adaptability, and an insatiable thirst for knowledge in fostering a mentality of constant growth.

Seeking Opportunities for Personal and Professional Development

In the legendary mindset, every experience is an opportunity for growth. Delve into the proactive approach that legendary individuals take in seeking opportunities for personal and professional development. Explore how challenges, successes, and even setbacks become stepping stones on the path to continual improvement.

Embracing Change as a Catalyst for Growth

Change is not a disruptor but a catalyst for growth in the legendary mindset. Explore how legendary individuals view change as an opportunity to learn, adapt, and evolve. Understand the role of resilience and a growth mindset in navigating the ever-shifting landscape of life with grace and purpose.

The Role of Mentorship in Lifelong Learning

Mentorship is a guiding light in the journey of continual growth. Delve into how legendary individuals seek and provide mentorship, creating a reciprocal relationship that fosters knowledge transfer and personal development. Explore the profound impact of mentorship on shaping the trajectory of a legendary mindset.

This section invites you to embrace the philosophy of continual growth and learning, recognizing it as a dynamic force within the legendary mindset that propels individuals toward enduring success and fulfillment.

Sub-Chapter 9.2 The Longevity of Success

Introduction

Embark on a reflective exploration of the longevity of success within the legendary mindset in this section titled "The Longevity of Success." For legendary individuals, success is not a fleeting moment but a sustained journey that withstands the tests of time. Delve into the principles and strategies that contribute to the enduring nature of success in the legendary mindset.

Cultivating Sustainable Habits for Success

Success is built on the foundation of sustainable habits. Explore how legendary individuals cultivate habits that contribute to their well-being, productivity, and overall success. Understand the role of discipline, time management, and self-care in creating a sustainable framework for long-term success.

Adapting to Evolving Challenges

Longevity of success requires the ability to adapt to evolving challenges. Delve into how legendary individuals navigate changes, setbacks, and external shifts with resilience and grace. Explore the mindset and strategies that contribute to sustained success in the face of a dynamic and ever-changing world.

Balancing Ambition and Contentment

Ambition fuels the journey, but contentment sustains it. Explore the delicate balance between ambition and contentment in the legendary mindset. Understand how legendary individuals set ambitious goals while appreciating and finding fulfillment in the present moment, creating a harmonious and lasting success.

Creating a Legacy of Impact

The longevity of success is intertwined with the impact left on the world. Delve into how legendary individuals go beyond personal success to create a legacy of positive influence and contribution. Explore the principles of ethical leadership, social responsibility, and community engagement that contribute to a meaningful and enduring legacy.

This section invites you to reflect on the principles that contribute to the longevity of success within the legendary mindset, recognizing it as a journey that extends far beyond individual achievements.

Sub-Chapter 9.3 Balancing Life and Success

Introduction

Embark on a thoughtful exploration of balancing life and success within the legendary mindset in this section titled "Balancing Life and Success." For legendary individuals, true success extends beyond professional achievements to encompass a harmonious integration of personal and professional life. Delve into the principles and practices that contribute to a balanced and fulfilling existence.

Defining Personal Values and Priorities

Balancing life and success begins with a clear understanding of personal values and priorities. Explore how legendary individuals define what truly matters to them, aligning their life choices with their core beliefs. Understand the role of self-reflection and intentional decision-making in creating a life that resonates with authenticity.

Effective Time Management for Well-Being

Time is a precious resource in the legendary mindset, and effective time management is key to a balanced life. Delve into the strategies legendary individuals employ to manage their time efficiently, ensuring that both personal and professional aspects receive the attention they deserve. Explore the art of prioritization and mindful scheduling.

Nurturing Relationships and Connections

True success is intertwined with meaningful relationships. Delve into how legendary individuals prioritize and nurture relationships with family, friends, and their broader network. Understand the role of empathy, communication, and quality time in fostering connections that contribute to a balanced and fulfilling life.

Wellness and Self-Care Practices

The legendary mindset recognizes the importance of wellness and self-care in sustaining success. Explore the wellness practices that legendary individuals incorporate into their daily lives, from physical fitness and mental well-being to

 moments of rejuvenation and self-reflection. Understand how prioritizing self-care contributes to overall life balance.

This section invites you to explore the principles and practices of balancing life and success within the legendary mindset, recognizing it as an integral aspect of a truly fulfilling and enduring journey.

Sub-Chapter 9.4 Passing the Legacy

Introduction

Embark on a contemplative exploration of passing the legacy within the legendary mindset in this section titled "Passing the Legacy." For legendary individuals, the journey of greatness extends beyond personal achievements to the meaningful transfer of knowledge, values, and inspiration to future generations. Delve into the principles and actions that contribute to passing on a legacy of impact and significance.

Mentorship as a Legacy-Building Tool

Mentorship is a powerful vehicle for passing on the legacy of wisdom and guidance. Explore how legendary individuals engage in mentorship, providing support and insights to those who follow in their footsteps. Understand the transformative impact of mentorship on shaping the next generation of leaders and thinkers.

Teaching and Sharing Knowledge

The legacy of knowledge is perpetuated through teaching and sharing. Delve into how legendary individuals actively participate in the dissemination of knowledge, whether through formal education, writing, or other forms of communication. Explore the role of knowledge-sharing in creating a ripple effect of intellectual and personal growth.

Fostering a Culture of Continuous Improvement

Passing the legacy involves instilling a commitment to continuous improvement. Explore how legendary individuals foster a culture within their teams and communities that values learning, innovation, and the pursuit of excellence. Understand how this commitment becomes an enduring legacy that shapes the mindset of future generations.

Community Engagement and Social Impact

The legacy of legendary individuals extends to the positive impact they create in society. Delve into how legendary individuals engage in community service, social causes, and philanthropy, leaving a legacy of compassion and positive change. Explore the role of social responsibility in passing on a legacy of significance.

This section invites you to reflect on the principles and actions that contribute to passing the legacy within the legendary mindset, recognizing it as a responsibility and an opportunity to shape the future for the better.

Sub-Chapter 9.5 The Unending Journey of a Legend

Introduction

Embark on a reflective exploration of the unending journey of a legend within the legendary mindset in this section titled "The Unending Journey of a Legend." For legendary individuals, the pursuit of greatness is not a destination but a continuous odyssey of growth, impact, and inspiration. Delve into the principles and perspectives that characterize the unending journey of a legend.

The Ever-Evolving Definition of Success

In the legendary mindset, success is not static but a concept that evolves with time and experience. Explore how legendary individuals embrace the fluidity of success, adapting their definition to align with their ever-evolving aspirations and values. Understand the role of self-awareness and reflection in shaping a personalized and meaningful definition of success.

Legacy as a Dynamic Concept

The legacy of a legend is not a fixed entity but a dynamic concept that adapts to changing contexts. Delve into how legendary individuals perceive and shape their legacy, recognizing that it is an ongoing narrative influenced by their actions, values, and impact. Explore the responsibility of continuously contributing to a positive and enduring legacy.

Embracing Challenges as Catalysts for Growth

The unending journey of a legend is marked by the embrace of challenges as opportunities for growth. Delve into how legendary individuals navigate setbacks, obstacles, and uncertainties with resilience and a growth mindset. Understand how challenges become catalysts for innovation, learning, and the continual evolution of a legendary mindset.

Inspiring Others on the Journey

The journey of a legend extends beyond personal success to the inspiration of others. Delve into how legendary individuals actively inspire and uplift those around them, fostering a culture of mentorship, collaboration, and shared success. Explore the ripple effect of inspiration as a transformative force in shaping the journeys of others.

This section invites you to contemplate the principles and perspectives that define the unending journey of a legend within the legendary mindset, recognizing it as a perpetual commitment to growth, impact, and the inspiration of future generations.

The end

Embrace the next level of transformation with our upcoming book, "The
Legendary Physique." While a legendary mindset lays the foundation for
greatness, a legendary physique completes the masterpiece. Unlock the secrets to
sculpting the body of your dreams, harmonizing strength, and achieving peak
physical condition. Elevate yourself to new heights of legendary living. Your
journey to greatness continues – stay tuned for the next chapter in the legendary
saga.

About the Author

The Trio: Guardians of Unity

In the mysterious world of authors, the Trio emerges as a powerful force, dedicated to shaping a future where masculinity and femininity harmonize, fostering unity and equality. Comprised of three enigmatic individuals, known collectively as the Trio, their identities shrouded in secrecy, they have embarked on a transformative journey to bring about positive change in society.

Mission and Purpose

The Trio's mission is profound yet simple — to revive the essence of manhood, womanhood, and the inherent qualities that make each individual unique. Their commitment extends beyond gender, encompassing the promotion of unity, equality, and respect for diverse beliefs. The Trio envisions a world where people coexist without prejudice, embracing the rich tapestry of humanity.

The Unveiling of Truths

With their first book, "Understanding the Legendary Mindset," the Trio invites readers on a quest for self-discovery and societal transformation. As staunch advocates for the fundamental values of respect, equality, and unity, the Trio aims to dismantle barriers and encourage open dialogue. This book is but the first step in a series dedicated to enlightening minds and inspiring positive change.

Beyond the Pages

The Trio's literary journey doesn't end here. Stay tuned for upcoming works that delve into the intricacies of life, relationships, and the pursuit of collective greatness. As the guardians of unity, the Trio invites you to join them in redefining societal narratives and embracing a future where every individual's uniqueness is celebrated.

Discover more about the Trio's vision, explore the legendary mindset, and embark on a transformative odyssey through the pages of their books. Together, let us unravel the mysteries of existence and forge a path towards a united and enlightened world.